Abraham Lincoln

Addressing a Nation

Torrey Maloof

Consultants

Vanessa Ann Gunther, Ph.D.
Department of History
Chapman University

Nicholas Baker, Ed.D.
Supervisor of Curriculum and Instruction
Colonial School District, DE

Katie Blomquist, Ed.S.
Fairfax County Public Schools

Publishing Credits

Rachelle Cracchiolo, M.S.Ed., *Publisher*
Conni Medina, M.A.Ed., *Managing Editor*
Emily R. Smith, M.A.Ed., *Series Developer*
Diana Kenney, M.A.Ed., NBCT, *Content Director*
Courtney Patterson, *Senior Graphic Designer*
Lynette Ordoñez, *Editor*

Image Credits: Cover page Culture Club/Getty Images; cover and p. 1 LOC [LC-DIG-ppmsca-19301]; p. 2 Kean Collection/Getty Images; pp. 4, 8, 9, 10 (left) Granger, NYC; p. 5 Sipley/ClassicStock/Getty Images; p. 6 Look and Learn/Bridgeman Images; p. 7 (top) LOC [LC-USZ62-56582], (bottom) George Eastman House/Getty Images; p. 10 (right) Record Group 11; General Records of the United States Government; National Archives; pp. 11, 18 (top) Bettmann/Getty Images; p. 12 Photo12/UIG via Getty Images; p. 13 (top) LOC [LC-USZC2-331], (bottom) LOC [LC-DIG-ppmsca-31540]; p. 14 Culture Club/Getty Images; pp. 15 (top), 17 North Wind Picture Archives; p. 15 (bottom) Niday Picture Library/Alamy Stock Photo; p. 16 LOC [LC-DIG-pga-02797]; p.18 (bottom) LOC [LC-USZ62-107689]; p. 19 (left) NARA [301682], (right) Kean Collection/Getty Images; pp. 20 (top), 23, 29 Ed Vebell/Getty Images, (bottom) LOC [LC-DIG-pga-07967]; p. 21 Manuscript Division, Library of Congress; p. 22 LOC [LC-USA7-16837]; p. 23 Public Domain/Wikimedia Commons; p. 24 Hulton Archive/Getty Images; p. 25 (top) LOC [lprbscsm.scsm0413], (bottom) LOC [LC-USZC4-5341]; pp. 28-29 The Abraham Lincoln Papers at the Library of Congress, Manuscript Division (Washington, D.C.: American Memory Project, [2000-02]); p. 32 LOC [LC-USZC4-5341]; back cover page LOC [LC-DIG-ppmsca-31540]; all other images from iStock and/or Shutterstock.

Library of Congress Cataloging-in-Publication Data

Names: Maloof, Torrey, author.
Title: Abraham Lincoln : addressing a nation / Torrey Maloof.
Description: Huntington Beach, CA : Teacher Created Materials, 2017. |
Includes index.
Identifiers: LCCN 2016034224 (print) | LCCN 2016034285 (ebook) | ISBN
9781493838059 (pbk.) | ISBN 9781480757707 (eBook)
Subjects: LCSH: Lincoln, Abraham, 1809-1865--Juvenile literature. |
Presidents--United States--Biography--Juvenile literature.
Classification: LCC E457.905 .M316 2017 (print) | LCC E457.905 (ebook) | DDC
973.7092 [B] --dc23
LC record available at https://lccn.loc.gov/2016034224

Teacher Created Materials
5301 Oceanus Drive
Huntington Beach, CA 92649-1030
http://www.tcmpub.com

ISBN 978-1-4938-3805-9

Printed by: 51497
Printed in: China

Table of Contents

The Great Emancipator

A young woman stands on a wooden platform at the front of a hot, crowded room. She is scared but stoic. She wears a clean dress that is not her own, and her hair has been roughly gathered and tucked under a bandana. All of a sudden, a man violently pulls her to the center of the stage as he yells out her age and weight. He boisterously informs the crowd that she is a hard worker. Men in the audience point at the woman as they whisper amongst themselves. Some come forward and poke her with canes while others feel her muscles with their hands. The crowd begins to yell out numbers. "Sold!" yells the man on stage. The woman's heart sinks for she knows she will never see her family again. She is a slave and has just been sold to a new master.

Slave auctions were a regular occurrence in New Orleans in the early 1800s. Enslaved people were shipped down the Mississippi River or marched along its banks in **coffle** gangs to be sold to **plantation** owners. A story goes that one day, a young man witnessed one of these slave auctions in New Orleans. The horrid spectacle haunted him for the rest of his life. His name was Abraham Lincoln, but he would later be known as the Great **Emancipator**.

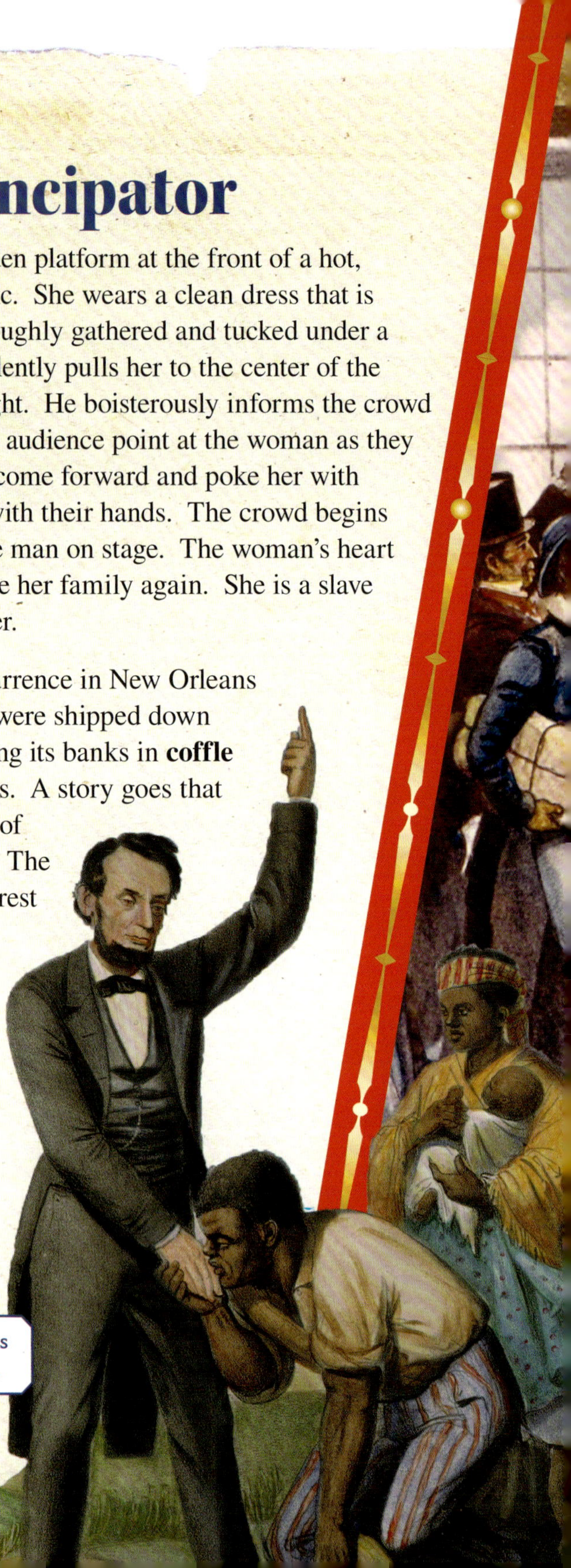

Lincoln is shown here as the Great Emancipator.

Lincoln observes a slave auction in New Orleans.

SLAVERY IN THE SOUTH

Enslaved people made up about one-third of the population in the **antebellum** South. They had no rights and no freedom. They weren't allowed to learn to read or write. Many were brutally beaten and punished regularly.

From the Frontier to Washington

On February 12, 1809, a baby boy named Abraham Lincoln was born in a simple log cabin deep in the woods of Kentucky. Lincoln's father was a hardworking farmer. His mother was a religious woman. She enjoyed reciting prayers and telling stories from the Bible to her newborn son and his older sister, Sarah. They were a happy family, but they were very poor.

When Lincoln was seven years old, the family had to move to another farm in Indiana. Lincoln worked hard on the family farm. He plowed, harvested, and split wood with an ax. He rarely attended school. There were not many schools on the **frontier**. Most children had to help out around the home. There was little time left for schooling. If Lincoln had any free time to himself, he spent it reading. He learned through his love of reading. He taught himself many subjects using any book or newspaper he could get his hands on.

ANIMAL LOVER

Lincoln loved animals. He had many pets growing up and many in the White House. Lincoln's wife once said her husband's favorite hobby was cats.

Lincoln studies by the fire.

At the age of nine, Lincoln was dealt a terrible blow. His mother, whom he loved dearly, passed away. Lincoln was heartbroken. But his father soon remarried, and Lincoln became very close with his new stepmother. She encouraged him to read and learn. He was always grateful for the love and attention she gave him.

the Lincoln cabin in Kentucky

Lincoln defends a man in court.

This 1850 photo shows the street where Lincoln's law office was located.

FAMILY MAN

Lincoln met Mary Ann Todd in Springfield. The two married in 1842 and had four children. Sadly, only one of their sons, Robert, lived to adulthood. Two children died before Lincoln did. Their sudden deaths were devastating for Lincoln.

In 1830, the Lincoln family moved to central Illinois. Lincoln helped his family build a new log cabin and start a farm. But after he turned 22, Lincoln left home. He did not want to be a farmer like his father. He longed for a different life. He said goodbye to his family and moved to New Salem, Illinois.

While in New Salem, Lincoln held all sorts of different jobs as he pondered what to do with his life. During this time, he also began his political career. He was elected to the Illinois General Assembly in 1834. It was one of the other representatives, John Todd Stuart, who suggested Lincoln become a lawyer. Lincoln liked the idea. He had long been interested in the law. Over the next three years, Lincoln studied law on his own. In 1837, he became a lawyer.

Lincoln was elected to four terms in the Assembly. During his third term, the capital of Illinois moved to Springfield. So in 1837, Lincoln moved, too. There, he joined Stuart's law office and became a very successful lawyer. He also improved his political skills. In 1846, he was elected to Congress. Once again, Lincoln was on the move. This time, he and his young family headed to Washington, DC.

The Little Giant vs. Long Abe

In 1849, Lincoln's term in Congress came to an end. He decided to move back to Illinois and practice law again. For five years, Lincoln steered clear of politics. But then came the Kansas-Nebraska Act. Lincoln was shocked by it. How could Congress pass this act?

Lincoln's old political rival, Stephen A. Douglas, was an Illinois state senator. In 1854, he introduced the Kansas-Nebraska Act. This act **repealed** the Missouri Compromise of 1820. Back then, Missouri was admitted to the United States as a slave state, while Maine was added as a free state. The Missouri Compromise balanced the number of free states and the number of slave states. It also said that any future states in the northern part of the Louisiana Territory would be added as free states. This would stop the spread of slavery. But Douglas's new act changed everything. The Kansas-Nebraska Act said that the settlers in those territories had the right to choose whether their state was going to be a slave state or a free state.

Lincoln had long detested slavery. He hoped that by stopping the spread of slavery, it would die out. But now, slavery was sure to spread west. Lincoln knew he had to throw his hat back in the political ring and fast. It was time to go after Douglas.

Kansas-Nebraska Act

Abraham Lincoln (left) and Stephen Douglas (right)

LINCOLN VS. DOUGLAS: THE EARLY YEARS

Lincoln and Douglas were from two different political parties. They disagreed on many things. The two men often debated. This made for a particularly comical scene because Douglas was much shorter than Lincoln.

In 1855, Lincoln ran for Douglas's Senate seat, but he lost. He spent the next two years traveling across Illinois giving antislavery speeches. He explained to audiences why he opposed slavery. He told them why the spread of slavery must be stopped. Lincoln believed in the immortal words of Thomas Jefferson. He quoted the Declaration of Independence: "All men are created equal." For Lincoln, this meant both black men and white men. It was his belief that *all* men deserved the right to "Life, Liberty, and the pursuit of Happiness."

Lincoln tried to win a Senate seat again in 1858. He went face to face with Douglas. The two men debated on the campaign trail over states' rights and slavery. The Lincoln-Douglas debates made national news. The whole country was watching. News reporters referred to the men as Long Abe and the Little Giant. The debates captivated the nation. Lincoln argued that slavery was morally wrong. Douglas argued that equal rights were for white men only. In the end, Douglas won the seat. But, Lincoln refused to give up. He was now a household name. His party believed he could be the next president. In 1860, they nominated him for the presidential election.

Lincoln speaks to a crowd in 1858.

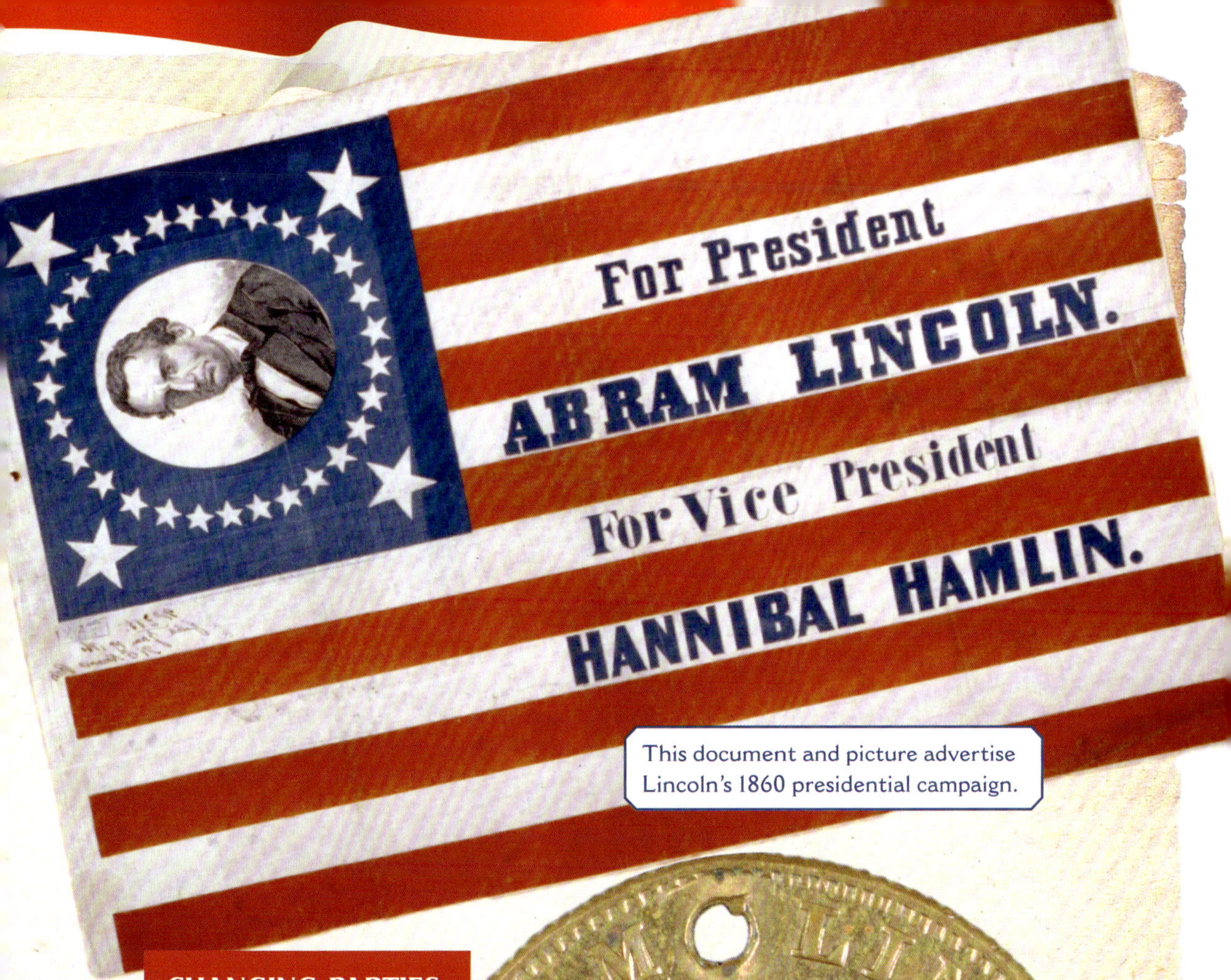

This document and picture advertise Lincoln's 1860 presidential campaign.

CHANGING PARTIES

In 1854, the Republican Party was formed. It firmly opposed the spread of slavery. Lincoln began his career in the Whig Party. In 1856, he became a Republican.

A House Divided

Two years prior to the election, Lincoln paraphrased the Bible. In one of his speeches he stated, "A house divided against itself cannot stand." He feared that slavery would tear the **Union** apart. Lincoln's words were **prophetic**. In November 1860, Lincoln beat Douglas. He was elected president. In December, before Lincoln took office, South Carolina **seceded** from the Union. Soon, other states followed.

On March 4, 1861, Lincoln gave his **inaugural** address. In his speech, he said he would not interfere with slavery in the South. He stressed the importance of keeping the Union together. He asked for both sides to compromise. Meanwhile, the people of the South were gathering supplies and building an army. They named their country the Confederate States of America. They even had their own president.

Lincoln is sworn in as president.

Confederates attack Fort Sumter.

On April 12, 1861, Lincoln's worst fears came true. The Confederates fired shots on Fort Sumter in South Carolina. The Civil War had begun. Lines were drawn. The North consisted of 23 states. The South had 11. Most leaders thought the war would be short. They were wrong.

WE WANT WHISKERS!

During the 1860 campaign, Lincoln received a letter from 11-year-old Grace Bedell. She said he would get more votes if he had a beard, or "whiskers." Lincoln took the girl's advice and grew a beard.

Lincoln had planned to let slavery exist in the South. But he wanted to prevent it from spreading west. He figured this way it would slowly die out. But more than a year into the war, Lincoln knew he had to change his plans.

Abolitionists had been pressuring Lincoln to free the enslaved people. But Lincoln was worried. There were four slave states that had not joined the Confederacy. They were the border states of Kentucky, Missouri, Maryland, and Delaware. Lincoln feared that these states would secede if he abolished slavery. He knew he needed their support to win the war. And he did not want to punish them for remaining loyal to the Union. Yet, the Union was struggling in the war. It was losing major battles to the South. Something had to be done.

In this 1888 print, Lincoln is shown above the Emancipation Proclamation.

Lincoln's cabinet helped him come to a resolution. He would free the slaves in the South, but not in the border states. The freed slaves could then fight for the Union and their freedom. This would strengthen the North and cripple the South. Lincoln waited until the North achieved its first big military victory. When General George McClellan defeated the Southern army at Antietam, Lincoln knew it was time. On September 22, 1862, he released the Emancipation Proclamation to the press.

FREDERICK DOUGLASS

Frederick Douglass was a famous abolitionist. He criticized the president for not ending slavery. But when the Emancipation Proclamation was released, Douglass was overjoyed. He said, "We shout for joy that we live to record this righteous decree."

Newly freed slaves walk to the North in 1863.

Battle of Gettysburg

In the summer of 1863, the Confederate army had pushed its way onto Northern soil. Southern troops invaded Pennsylvania. Union forces rushed to stop them. The two sides met in the small town of Gettysburg. More than 165,000 soldiers fought for three days. In the end, the Union army won. But, the win came at a large cost. There were more than 51,000 **casualties**.

This 1863 photo shows Lincoln in a crowd at Gettysburg.

Four months after the battle, people were still burying the dead. A new cemetery was built on the battlefield. President Lincoln was invited to the cemetery's dedication on November 19. He was asked to deliver a few words to honor the fallen Union soldiers. He wrote a brief speech. It was only 272 words.

The first speaker at the dedication was Edward Everett. He was a famous **orator**. He spoke for two hours. Then, Lincoln took the stage. He took his speech out of his pocket, put on his glasses and began, "Four score and seven years ago our fathers brought forth upon this continent, a new nation, conceived in liberty, and dedicated to the proposition that all men are created equal."

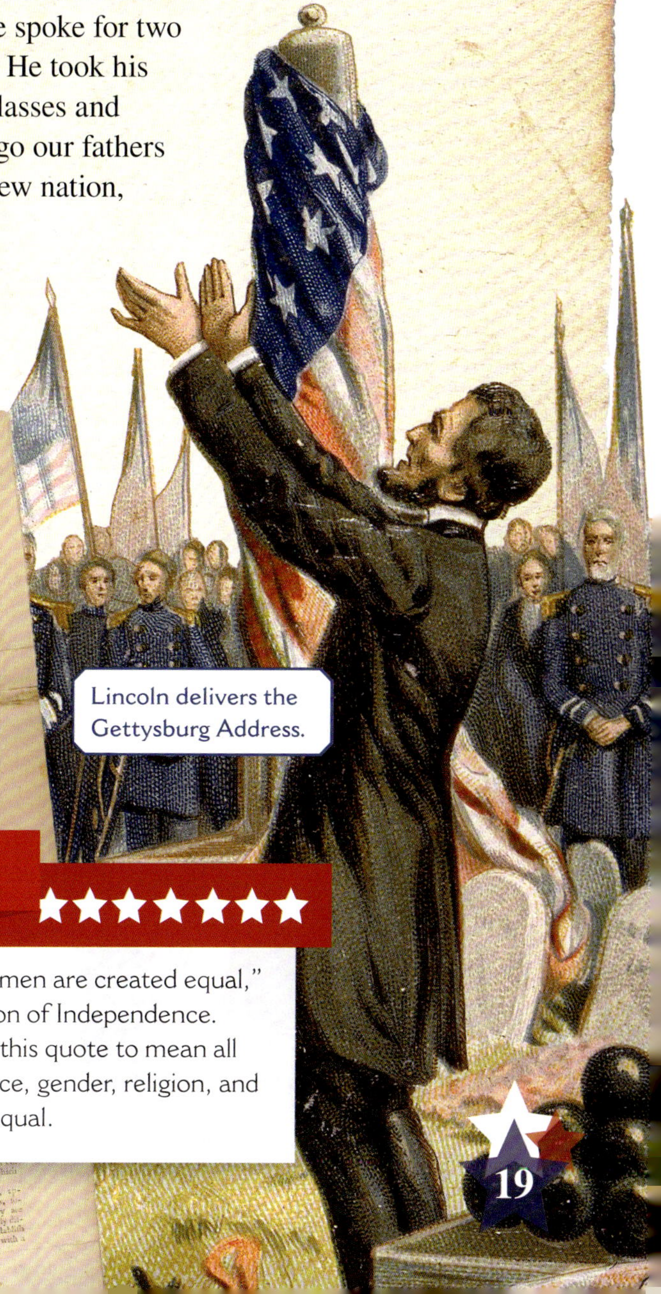

Lincoln delivers the Gettysburg Address.

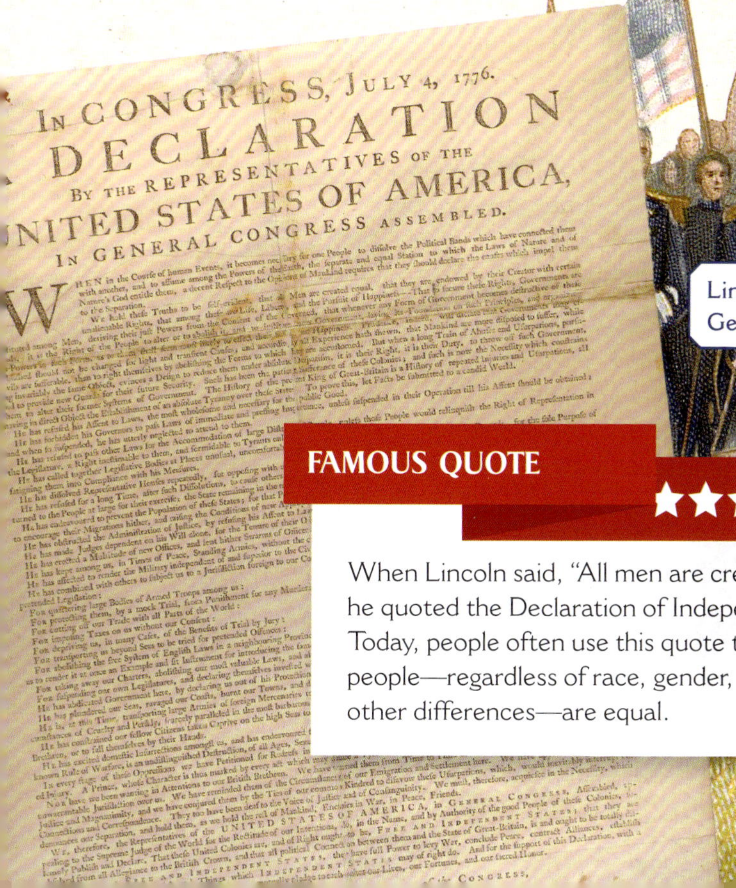
IN CONGRESS, JULY 4, 1776.
A DECLARATION
BY THE REPRESENTATIVES OF THE
UNITED STATES OF AMERICA,
IN GENERAL CONGRESS ASSEMBLED.

FAMOUS QUOTE

When Lincoln said, "All men are created equal," he quoted the Declaration of Independence. Today, people often use this quote to mean all people—regardless of race, gender, religion, and other differences—are equal.

In just two minutes, Lincoln had redefined the war. He reminded people that the country was founded on liberty and equality. He said that the Civil War was a test to see if a nation based on these principles could survive. It was a war to save democracy. Lincoln urged the people to finish the task at hand. If they did, then the "government of the people, by the people, and for the people" would not disappear or "perish from the earth."

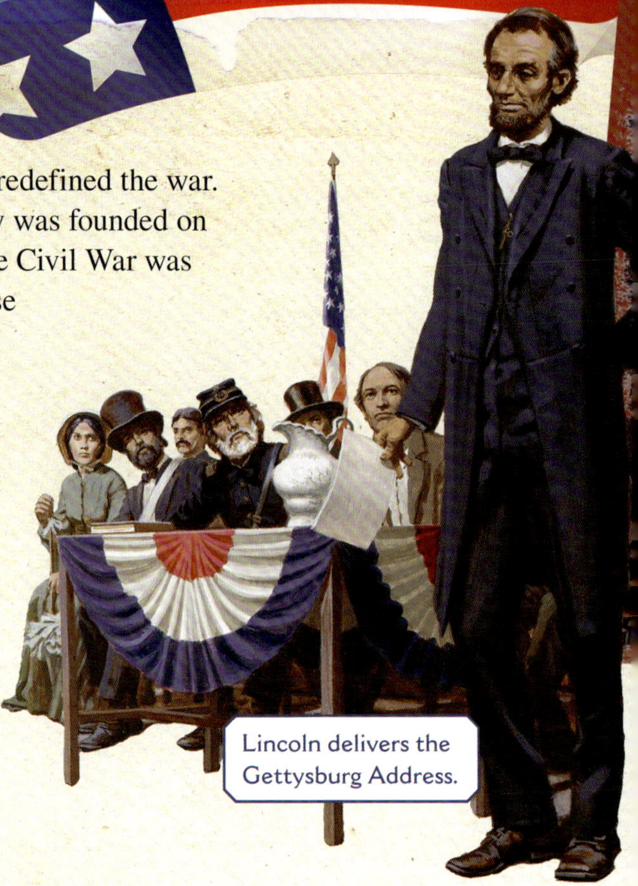

Lincoln delivers the Gettysburg Address.

In 1864, the war was still raging. Many lives were being lost daily and there seemed to be no end in sight. To make matters worse, Lincoln's first term as president was coming to an end. He would soon have to run for re-election. It was not going to be easy. Even his own party did not think he could win the election. Lincoln was beginning to think the same. But then, something amazing happened.

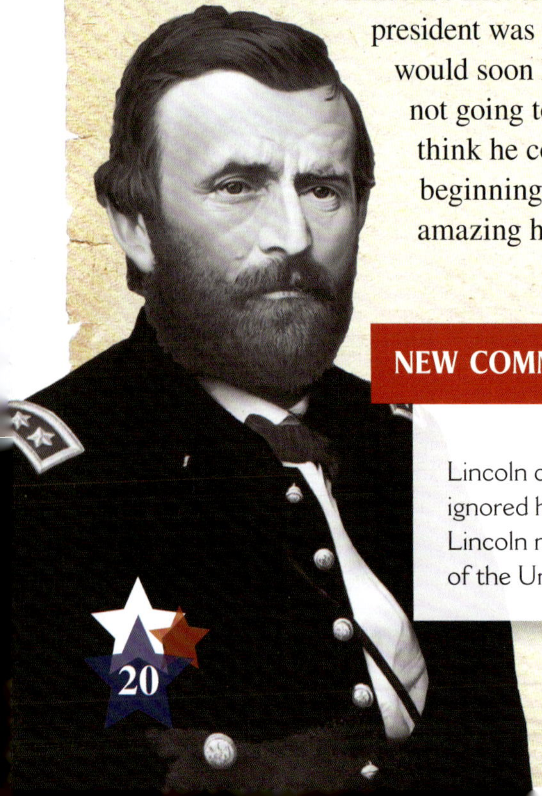

NEW COMMANDER

Lincoln changed generals many times. They often ignored his orders and acted on their own. In 1864, Lincoln made General Ulysses S. Grant commander of the Union army. It proved to be a good choice.

Battle of Atlanta

Union troops captured the city of Atlanta. It was one of the most important cities in the South. It served as a key transportation center for the Confederate army. In September, Union General William T. Sherman sent a telegram to Lincoln stating, "Atlanta is ours, and fairly won."

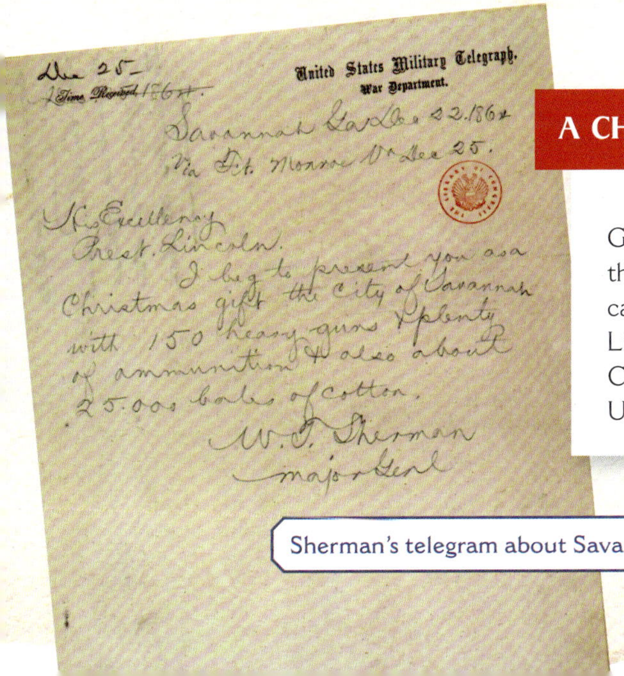

Dec 25
Time Received 186
United States Military Telegraph.
War Department.
Savannah Ga Dec 22 1864
Via Ft Monroe Va Dec 25.
His Excellency
Prest. Lincoln.
I beg to present you as a Christmas gift the City of Savannah with 150 heavy guns & plenty of ammunition & also about 25,000 bales of cotton.
W. T. Sherman
Major Genl

Sherman's telegram about Savannah

A CHRISTMAS GIFT

General Sherman continued to march through Georgia. In December, he captured Savannah. In a telegram to Lincoln, he called the captured city a Christmas gift for the president. The Union army was on its way to victory.

When it came time for the election, a Union victory was well within reach. Because of this, Lincoln easily won. With the war under control, Lincoln returned his attention to the issue of slavery. He knew the Emancipation Proclamation was not enough. He wanted an amendment to the Constitution. It would abolish slavery once and for all. In January of 1865, the House of Representatives voted to pass the 13th Amendment. By the end of the year it would be **ratified**. Slavery would be abolished.

On March 4, 1865, people gathered in front of the Capitol. They were there to hear Lincoln give his second inaugural address. The sun peeked through the clouds as Lincoln began to speak. He talked about the evils of slavery. He said the war was God's punishment for slavery. He urged forgiveness. He did not want to punish the South. Rather, he wanted to focus on healing. He wanted to bind the nation's wounds. He argued for **Reconstruction**, not retaliation.

Lincoln gives his second inaugural address.

General Lee surrenders in Appomattox Court House, Virginia.

By April, the Union army was in Virginia. They had the enemy trapped. Confederate General Robert E. Lee had no choice. He requested a meeting with Grant. The two men met on April 9. Lee **surrendered**. Other Confederate leaders followed over the next few months. The Civil War was over and the Union had won.

1861

THE STRESS OF WAR

Lincoln aged dramatically during the war. His cheeks sunk as lines and wrinkles deeply etched their way into his face. The stress of war took a great toll on the president.

1865

Untimely Death

Lincoln had long been fascinated by the meaning of dreams. Just a few days after Lee's surrender, Lincoln had a dream, which he shared with his wife and a small group of friends. He told them that in his dream he heard sobbing in the White House. He followed the sorrowful cries to the East Room where he found a covered corpse surrounded by soldiers and mourners. Lincoln asked one of the soldiers, "Who is dead in the White House?" The soldier replied, "The president. He was killed by an **assassin**."

On April 14, 1865, Lincoln was feeling relieved and happy that the war was over. He headed to Ford's Theatre to see a play with his wife. At the theater, Lincoln sat in a rocking chair in the president's box. Mary sat by Lincoln's side holding his arm. During the third act, a man burst into the box and shot Lincoln in the back of the head. Mary screamed as the assassin, the famous actor John Wilkes Booth, escaped the theater.

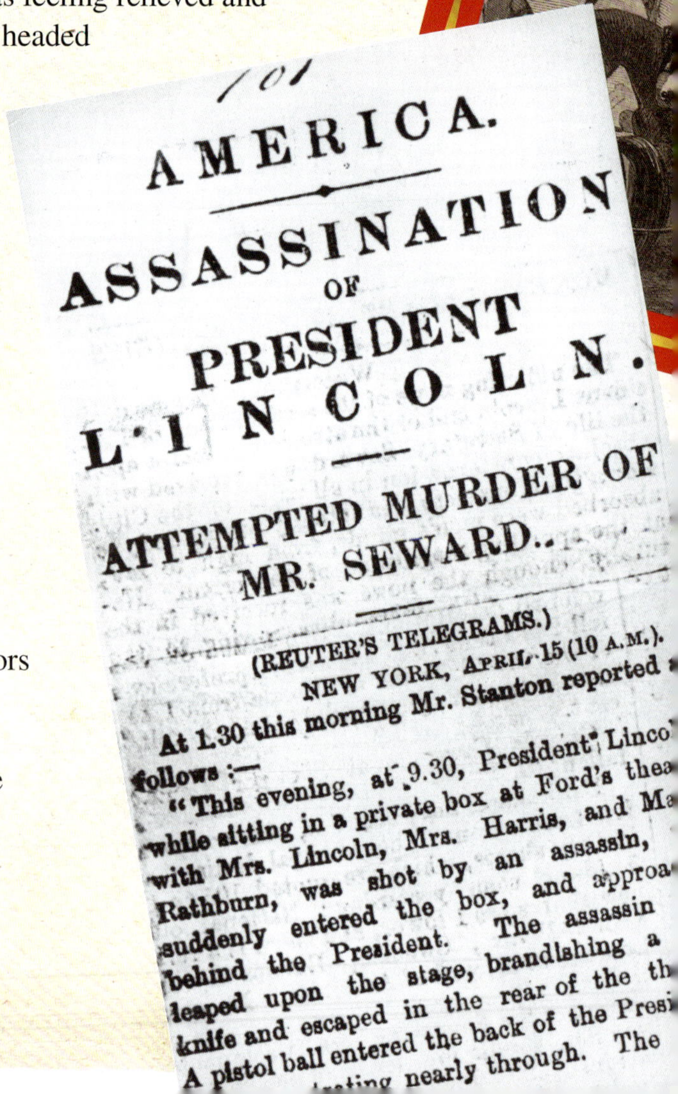

101

AMERICA.

ASSASSINATION OF PRESIDENT LINCOLN.

ATTEMPTED MURDER OF MR. SEWARD.

(REUTER'S TELEGRAMS.)

NEW YORK, April 15 (10 A.M.).

At 1.30 this morning Mr. Stanton reported follows :—

"This evening, at 9.30, President Linco while sitting in a private box at Ford's thea with Mrs. Lincoln, Mrs. Harris, and Ma Rathburn, was shot by an assassin, suddenly entered the box, and approa behind the President. The assassin leaped upon the stage, brandishing a knife and escaped in the rear of the th A pistol ball entered the back of the Presi nearly through. The

Soldiers carried the mortally wounded president across the street to a boarding house. Doctors worked on the president all night but could not save him. Lincoln died at 7:22 a.m. on April 15. He was 56 years old.

Lincoln's funeral procession

SURRAT. BOOTH.

War Department, Washington, April 20,

$100,000 REWARD!

THE MURDERER

Of our late beloved President, Abraham Lincoln,

IS STILL AT LARGE.

$50,000 REWARD

Will be paid by this Department for his apprehension, in addition to any reward offered by Municipal Authorities or State Executives.

$25,000 REWARD

Will be paid for the apprehension of JOHN H. SURRATT, one of Booth's Accomplices.

$25,000 REWARD

Will be paid for the apprehension of David C. Harold, another of Booth's accomplices.

BOOTH'S ESCAPE

Booth managed to escape the theater. Federal troops found him 12 days later. He was shot to death when he tried to get away. The other **conspirators** who helped Booth plan the assassination were also found and tried for their crimes.

Now He Belongs to the Ages

Lincoln's death shocked the nation. People poured into Washington, DC, to mourn the fallen president. On April 21, Lincoln's body was placed on a train. The train traveled to Illinois where his body was laid to rest. Along the way, the train stopped in 12 cities. It is estimated that seven million Americans paid their respects to the Great Emancipator.

Lincoln's tomb in Springfield, Illinois

After Lincoln took his last breath, it is said that Secretary of War Edwin M. Stanton whispered, "Now he belongs to the ages." Stanton's **epitaph** was fittingly perfect. Lincoln does belong to the ages. He belongs to history. His legacy lives on. He has become an almost mythical figure. He was a poor, backwoods boy who grew up to be president. He led the Union during a brutal and bloody war. He believed with all his heart that "all men are created equal." In truth, he lived and died for that belief. Lincoln was a hero for his time and a president for the ages.

Lincoln memorial in Washington, DC

Rewrite It!

Abraham Lincoln gave many powerful speeches during his lifetime. But his most famous speech is the Gettysburg Address. Those 272 words not only honored fallen soldiers but also gave purpose to a brutal and bloody war.

Read Lincoln's Gettysburg Address. Look up words you do not understand. Then, rewrite it in your own words. Be sure to keep the meaning of the speech the same. Recite your speech for your family and friends. Share what you learned about President Lincoln and what the Gettysburg Address means to you.

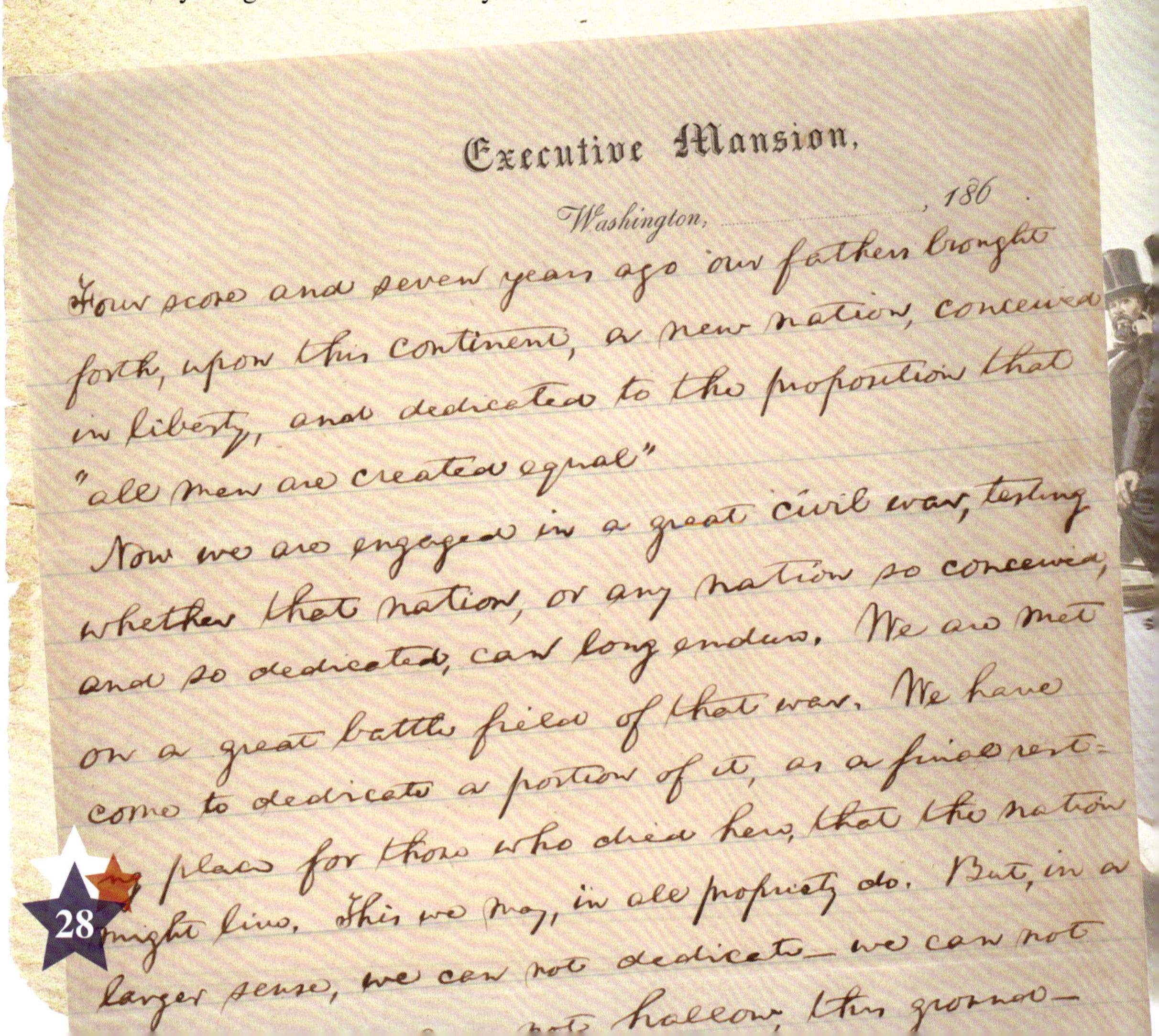
Executive Mansion,

Washington, , 186

Four score and seven years ago our fathers brought forth, upon this continent, a new nation, conceived in liberty, and dedicated to the proposition that "all men are created equal"

Now we are engaged in a great civil war, testing whether that nation, or any nation so conceived, and so dedicated, can long endure. We are met on a great battle field of that war. We have come to dedicate a portion of it, as a final resting place for those who died here, that the nation might live. This we may, in all propriety do. But, in a larger sense, we can not dedicate— we can not hallow, this ground—

"all men are created equal"

Glossary

abolitionists—people who were against slavery and worked to end it

antebellum—occurring in the Southern United States before the Civil War

assassin—a person who kills a famous or important person, usually for political reasons or money

casualties—people who are hurt or killed during an accident or war

coffle—a line of slaves bound together by chains

conspirators—people who are involved in a secret plan to do something harmful or illegal

emancipator—a person who frees someone or something from another person's control or power

epitaph—something written or said in memory of a dead person

frontier—an area where few people live

inaugural—part of an official ceremony in which a person is newly elected to an office

orator—a skillful public speaker who gives powerful speeches

plantation—a large farm that produces crops for money

prophetic—saying or foretelling what will happen in the future

ratified—made official through signing or voting

Reconstruction—the period after the Civil War in which the U.S. government attempted to admit the Confederate states back into the Union and resolve issues pertaining to freed slaves

repealed—thrown out, canceled

seceded—formally separated from a nation or state

surrendered—agreed to stop fighting because you knew you would not win

Union—term used to describe the United States of America; also the name given to the Northern army during the Civil War

Index

Your Turn!

SURRAT. BOOTH. HAROLD.

War Department, Washington, April 20, 1865,

$100,000 REWARD!

THE MURDERER

Of our late beloved President, Abraham Lincoln,

IS STILL AT LARGE.

$50,000 REWARD

Will be paid by this Department for his apprehension, in addition to any reward offered by Municipal Authorities or State Executives.

$25,000 REWARD

Will be paid for the apprehension of JOHN H. SURRATT, one of Booth's Accomplices.

$25,000 REWARD

Will be paid for the apprehension of David C. Harold, another of Booth's accomplices.

EDWIN M. STANTON, Secretary of War.

Reward!

The 1865 document above lists rewards for John Wilkes Booth and other people who conspired to assassinate Lincoln. How does this document show Americans' feelings about Lincoln in 1865? How do you know? Write a short paragraph to answer these questions.